GHOSTBUSTERS COLLECTABLES

Matt MacNabb

AMBERLEY

First published 2016

Amberley Publishing
The Hill, Stroud
Gloucestershire, GL5 4EP

www.amberley-books.com

Copyright © Matt MacNabb, 2016

The right of Matt MacNabb to be identified as the
Author of this work has been asserted in accordance
with the Copyrights, Designs and Patents Act 1988.

ISBN 978 1 4456 5430 0 (print)
ISBN 978 1 4456 5431 7 (ebook)

British Library Cataloguing in Publication Data.
A catalogue record for this book is available from
the British Library.

Typeset in 10pt on 13pt Celeste.
Typesetting by Amberley Publishing.
Printed in the UK.

Contents

Acknowledgments

The author would like to thank the following people for their assistance, without which this book would not have been possible. Thank you to Dan Aykroyd for being gracious enough to take time out of his busy schedule to write the foreword for this book, and thank you to Susan Patricola for helping to make it happen. Your contribution is this fan's dream come true. A special thanks to my good friend and super collector, Robert Barbieri, for the use of his impressive and extensive Ghostbusters collection for many of the photos. Your hard work and dedication enriched this showcase to another level. Thanks also to Jonathan Shyman for the use of images from his rare *Extreme Ghostbusters* unproduced and prototype collection. A big shout out to Yoko McCann at Funko, Zach Oat at Diamond Select Toys and Ashley Edwards at Flash Point PR/Lego for your contributions. Finally, thank you to my supportive and wonderful family: my wife Holly and our children Sebastian, Anastasia, Alexandre and Callidora. You are my world.

Foreword
by Dan Aykroyd

One of the thrilling experiences when I worked on *Ghostbusters* along with Ivan, Bill, Ernie, Rick, Sigourney and Harold were the meetings on set when all the brilliant ideas from toymakers would be presented. Truly great minds, talents and inspired manufacturing processes went into every Ghostbusters item. Who can forget the Toilet Bowl Ghost or the Transforming Volkswagen Bug?

Here now, for everyone and especially for the serious collector, is the definitive compendium of Ghostbusters merchandise produced throughout the life of the concept to date across a spectrum of applications by at least two generations of the most innovative and smartest designers and fabricators in the industry.

Introduction

The year was 1984 and the landscape of American cinema was rapidly changing and evolving. It turned out to be a landmark year for moviegoers, with the release of now-cult films like *Gremlins, Karate Kid, Beverly Hills Cop, Police Academy, Sixteen Candles, The NeverEnding Story* and *The Terminator*, just to name a few. One fateful day – 8 June 1984 to be exact – a new and fresh movie hit the cinemas. The tale of three somewhat eccentric and underappreciated parapsychologists who manage to be at the right place at the right time and with the right tools. The three morph from the practice of simply studying and hunting ghosts to a full-on ghost-catching business. New York City just happens to be on the precipice of a major paranormal event, so ghosts are literally crawling out of the woodwork. The trio eventually get so overworked that they hire a fourth Ghostbuster, battle a giant Marshmallow Man and a living god in the heart of New York City, and history was born.

In curating this book showcasing Ghostbusters collectables, I took painstaking care to select items that I felt were the best representations of the franchise over the years. Obviously, we couldn't include every single item in the book, but I hope that what I have squeezed into these pages will bring you as much joy and fond memories as I experienced in creating it. Those of us that grew up in the *Ghostbusters* era all have particular items that we fancy more than others. There are those of us that prefer the Kenner toys, others are into the Hi-C Ecto Cooler items, while some may feel more connected to the cereal toys. Whatever your passion, I'm confident that this book has something for everyone.

I have spent several years developing the collector website GhostbustersCollector.com (formerly GBCollector.com). I continue to work on adding to the website, but like many children of the 1980s, sometimes it's just nice to hold something physical in my hands to enjoy, and that's where this book comes in. *Ghostbusters Collectables* serves as a wonderful companion piece to GhostbustersCollector.com and will hopefully bring you as much joy as these toys bring me.

Chapter One
Ghostbusters: The 1984 Feature Film

The landscape of American cinema and pop culture both changed drastically on one fateful day – 8 June 1984. The day that *Ghostbusters* exploded into theaters had a profound impact. It's been over thirty years and fans are still celebrating this now-classic supernatural comedy film, which continues to resonate so very strongly.

It feels like a given now, but back in 1984 there were no movies about ghost hunters and certainly none that took the topic even remotely seriously. Filmation had produced a live-action series in the 1970s with the same title, featuring two goofy ghost hunters and their gorilla friend. Fans would later see that concept turned into a competing cartoon in 1986.

The beauty of *Ghostbusters* was the mixture of horror and comedy, which almost felt legitimate in some way. The concept for *Ghostbusters* was developed originally by the comedic and creative genius of Dan Aykroyd and Harold Ramis, the actors that portrayed Ray Stantz and Egon Spengler in the film. The film was masterfully produced and directed by Ivan Reitman, who had worked previously with Bill Murray and Harold Ramis on the cult comedy hit *Stripes*. The film was intended to consist of a mixture of *Saturday Night Live* alumni, such as John Belushi and Eddie Murphy, and other great comedic actors such as John Candy. Belushi passed away before he could fulfill the role of Peter Venkman and John Candy wouldn't commit to portraying Louis Tully. Eddie Murphy went the route of *Beverly Hills Cop*, a film that would spawn a franchise for him and make him a huge star of cinema. It all worked out for the best, because in the end fans got what is now a beloved cast of characters, portrayed by just the right mixture of actors.

The Ghostbusters merchandise train really took off in 1986 with the inception of the Kenner toy line based on *The Real Ghostbusters*, an animated series based on the 1984 feature film. There was a fair amount of merchandise produced for the first film, but a good majority of it was practical items such as t-shirts, stickers, buttons, posters and books. This was during an era when iron-on t-shirt shops were still a huge trend, so a lot of licensed shirts from the era can be found in a variety of shirt colors. Ghostbusters movie shirts of the era can be seen on everything from black to purple to red t-shirts. The best-selling collectable from the original film would no doubt be the single of the theme song by Ray Parker Jr. It was released on both record and cassette tape.

In the modern era, toy companies have done their best to make up the gap that we always had with the first film by producing a variety of classic film themed items. We will cover those in later chapters of the book. In the meantime, please enjoy this sampling of collectables from the very first *Ghostbusters* film.

Ghostbusters Canned Ghost
This promotional gimmick item was released to promote the first film. They are often a hard-to-find collectable today.

Ghostbusters Super Jumbo Floor Puzzle
This giant floor puzzle, produced by Jaymar, features forty-nine pieces and was one of the few mass-market items released for the original film. The puzzle features various images of the three original Ghostbusters from the movie poster and ghosts like Gozer, Stay Puft, Slimer, one of the Terror Dogs and more.

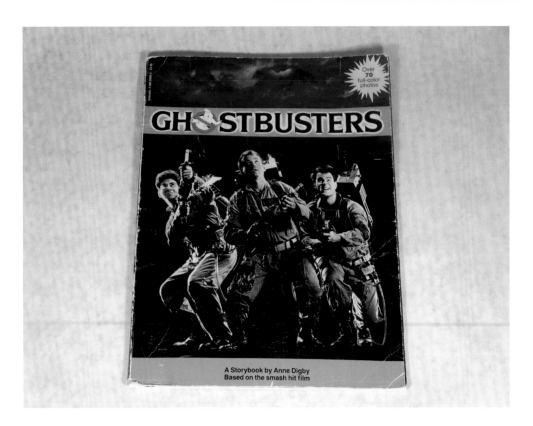

Ghostbusters Oversized Storybook
This softcover storybook, adapted by Anne Digby, includes seventy color photos from the feature film and an adaptation of the story. This book was one of the few book releases associated with the film at mass retail, and is thus rather prolific on the secondary market even today.

Ghostbusters Haunted House Activity Book
Scholastic released this activity book in conjunction with the original feature film. This rare coloring and activity book can be very difficult to come by on the secondary market today.

Ghostbusters **Picture Disc Record**
This record of Ray Parker Jr's hit *Ghostbusters* movie theme song was released at one point as a special edition picture disc.

Ghostbusters **Movie Promotional Stickers**
These promotional stickers were given out to promote the 1984 *Ghostbusters* feature film.

***Ghostbusters Meet the Laser Ghost* Book and Cassette Tape**
This Peter Pan produced storybook is a rare example of an illustrated book that actually features the likenesses of the actors from the 1984 film.

Fright Flicks Horror Trading Cards
The Topps trading card company released this set of cards from various 1980s horror and sci-fi films with silly captions underneath. There are three Ghostbusters cards in the line and the stickers come together to make a scene that includes both Slimer and the Library Ghost.

The Official Ghostbusters *Training Manual,* Movie Book and *The Story Behind* Ghostbusters
Books
'A Guide to Catching Ghosts' – this fun training manual included twelve stickers and a certificate at the end of the book for kids to hang on their wall. The *Ghostbusters* movie book is a brief recap of the film with stickers, and *The Story Behind Ghostbusters* gave kids a look into the making of the film. These half-size books could be found at retail and through school book orders.

Ghostbusters Book Ownership Sticker
These book stickers were a common giveaway item in the 1980s. They were often provided by libraries and can be extremely difficult to find.

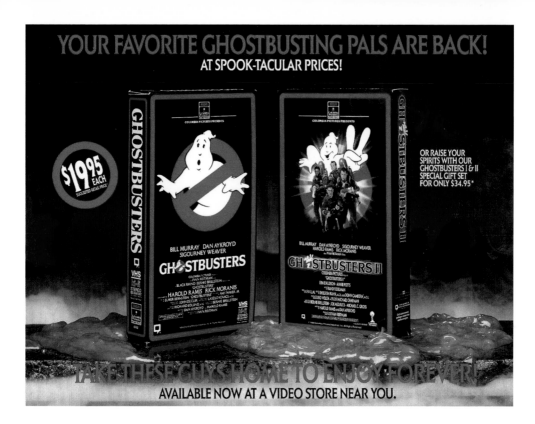

Ghostbusters VHS

This film was released on VHS in an era when home video was still a new and exciting format. The movie remained expensive until the release of *Ghostbusters II*, when it was re-released and also included in a two-pack.

Ghostbusters Video Game

Ghostbusters was given the video game treatment, produced by Activision. *Ghostbusters* movie games would be produced for the Atari 800, Atari 2600, Sega Master System, Commodore 64 and Nintendo platforms. There was a different version of the game produced later for the Sega Mega Drive/Genesis.

Ralston Ghostbusters Cereal

The initial release of this cereal was prior to the launch of *The Real Ghostbusters* cartoon. This version of the cereal offered a variety of in-pack prizes from a piece of Bazooka bubble gum to a frisbee flyer. There was also a mail-in offer on the boxes for a Ghostbuster kit. If kids sent in $1.50, they could get this 'official Ghostbuster gear': 11 inch × 14 inch poster ('Back Off Man! I'm a Ghostbuster'), one glow-in-the-dark door sign sticker, one glow-in-the-dark light switch cover, two sheets of Ghostbuster stickers, Ghostbuster button and an official Ghostbuster membership certificate.

Chapter Two
The Real Ghostbusters Cartoon

Following the success of the 1984 *Ghostbusters* feature film, Columbia decided that they wanted to continue the momentum of the brand by expanding it into an animated series. They approached DIC to handle the animation and sold the show to ABC. The series debuted in 1986 and was a smash hit. The series ended up airing six days a week in its prime. *The Real Ghostbusters* was the number-one-rated ABC Saturday morning cartoon during the height of its run and even ranked in the top five Saturday morning cartoons overall.

This cartoon was so important to the Ghostbusters franchise because it was what really fleshed out the characters for kids and kept the franchise alive for so many years in-between the two feature films and even years after *Ghostbusters II*. The cartoon also spawned the most merchandise and brought in a lot of new fans, even those too young to have seen the original film in theaters. The series was so popular that surveys of the era showed that 90 per cent of kids in the United States were aware of and liked *The Real Ghostbusters*! That's an astounding figure.

Kenner, the company that had made its name producing the Star Wars movie toy lines, were awarded the license to produce the action figures, vehicles, playsets and roleplay items. In the Christmas of 1987, the Kenner *The Real Ghostbusters* toys were ranked in the top five selling toys for the holiday season, and were even sold out in many areas. They remain favorites among fans and collectors and, in fact, are the most collected aspect of the Ghostbusters franchise.

The toy line ended rather abruptly due to an overwhelming turn in popularity among children towards the *Teenage Mutant Ninja Turtles*. There was a final proposed line of toys that was to include a wave of action figures titled the 'Backpack Heroes'. This wave of figures was only featured in the 1991 'Kenner – Hot, Hot, Hot' toy fair promotional booklet. The wave was to consist of the four main Ghostbusters, all in the standard original mold, but each in a solid color: Winston (Purple), Egon (Red), Ray (Orange) and Peter (Green), with a 'No-Ghost' logo on the chest. The figures each had a Containment Unit Backpack that could contain or launch their ghosts.

The Real Ghostbusters Wave One

The initial wave of the Kenner *The Real Ghostbusters* line began hitting shelves in 1986 and could be found there in various pressings for about a year. This would be the first and last time that kids could capture their favorite ghost hunters in their cartoon-accurate colored costumes. The figures each came with a Proton Pack (and obnoxiously long Nutrona beam) and a ghost. Included were Egon (Gulper Ghost), Peter (Grabber Ghost), Ray (Wrapper Ghost) and Winston (Chomper Ghost).

The Real Ghostbusters Wave Two (Fright Features)
This second wave of action figures allowed kids to press on an arm and give their toy a cartoonish mechanized fright expression. This wave featured the first ever Janine figure. The figures each came with a special weapon and ghost: Peter (Hook Shot Weapon/Gruesome Twosome Ghost), Egon (Terror Tweezer Weapon/Sour Throat Ghost), Ray (Fork Lift Weapon/Jail Jaw Ghost), Winston (Spud Thud Weapon/Scream Roller Ghost) and Janine (Unnamed Weapon/Boo Fish Ghost).

The Real Ghostbusters Wave Three (Super Fright Features)
The third wave of figures, dubbed Super Fright Features, built upon the concept of the second wave. Included were Janine (Unnamed Weapon/Boo Fish Ghost), Peter (Unnamed Weapon/Snake Head Ghost), Ray (Unnamed Weapon/Monster Mouth Ghost), Egon (Unnamed Weapon/Slimy Spider Ghost) and Winston (Unnamed Weapon/Meanie Weenie Ghost).

The Real Ghostbusters Wave Four (Screaming Heroes)
This wave of figures each came packed with a plastic ghost that kids could use to wind the figure up and activate an action feature, like spinning head, legs or arms: Peter (Laser Light Weapon/ Ghost Trap/Ghoulgroan Ghost), Egon (Mini-Harpoon Weapon/PKE Meter/Squidsqueal Ghost), Ray (Radar Ray Weapon/Vermoan Ghost), Winston (Proton Pistol Weapon/Houndhowl Ghost) and Janine (Purple Probe Weapon/Ghost Talker/Swinewhine Ghost).

The Real Ghostbusters Wave Five (Power Pack Heroes)
The Power Pack Heroes wave gave kids the very first Louis Tully figure and the very first standard-sculpt Janine figure. This wave also saw the re-release of the original molds of the figures for the first time since 1986. These redecos featured new color schemes and each had a backpack-style attachment that added an accessory. Pictured here are Egon (Crazy Copter/ Twister Ghost), Peter (Bouncin' Bazooka/Lightning Ghost), Ray (Grabbin' Grappler/Snatcher Ghost), Winston (Cyclin' Slicer/Splitting Ghost), Louis (Power Pincher/Vapor Ghost) and Janine (Racin' Wringer/Stretch Ghost).

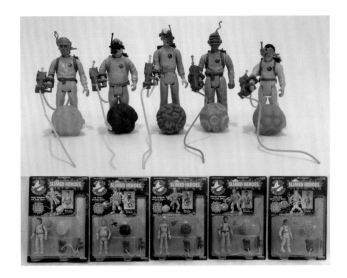

***The Real Ghostbusters* Wave Six (Slimed Heroes)**
This wave of figures again utilized the classic original mold and re-released the original Proton Packs, this time in a purple deco. The figures all came with a ghost, which kids used to squirt cold water on the toys, making 'slime' appear. A squirt of warm water would then erase the slime. Pictured here are Egon (Proton Blaster, Proton Pack and Mask/Brain Ghost), Ray (Proton Blaster, Proton Pack and Mask/Vapor Ghost), Peter (Proton Blaster, Proton Pack and Mask/Teeth Ghost), Winston (Proton Blaster, Proton Pack and Mask/Sucker Ghost) and Louis (Proton Blaster, Proton Pack and Mask/Four-Eyed Ghost).

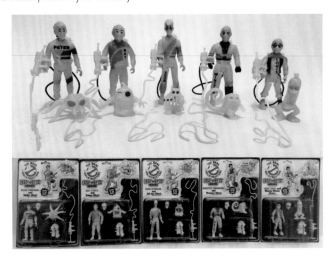

***The Real Ghostbusters* Wave Seven (Ecto-Glow Heroes)**
The final wave of *Real Ghostbusters* figures was released in 1991. Due to stiff competition with other franchises, like *Teenage Mutant Ninja Turtles*, the toys and cartoon were no longer able to survive in the marketplace. This wave again featured the original sculpts, this time decorated in neon colors and a glow-in-the-dark deco. Pictured are Egon (Proton Blaster/Proton Pack and Spare Head/Jail Jaw Ghost), Ray (Proton Blaster, Proton Pack and Spare Head/Gulper Ghost), Peter (Proton Blaster, Proton Pack and Spare Head/Slimey Spider Ghost), Winston (Proton Blaster, Proton Pack and Spare Head/Wrapper Ghost) and Louis (Proton Blaster, Proton Pack and Spare Head/Meanie Weenie Ghost).

The Real Ghostbusters
Green Ghost
The 'Green Ghost' was one
of the first ghost figures
to be released by Kenner.
Fans know him as 'Slimer'
but, before the cartoon
took off, there were only
the movie nicknames
for the ghost, which were
the Green Ghost, the
Onionhead Ghost and the
Ugly Little Spud.

The Real Ghostbusters
**Stay Puft Marshmallow
Man**
The Stay Puft
Marshmallow Man was
also released early in
the toy line. Kenner
opted to make a vastly
scaled-down version,
frustrating children
everywhere! This figure
has a variant, which
features a card back
dedicated to Kroger
grocery stores.

The Real Ghostbusters H2Ghost
'2 Ghosts In One! Each Squirts Water!'
This blue ghost comes apart into two
pieces and squirts water. This was one of
the first original Kenner designs that was
not taken from the cartoon or movies.

The Real Ghostbusters Fearsome Flush
Oh yeah, it's a ghost toilet. Perhaps you
had to be there back in the eighties, but
this ghost was always a lot of fun. He
appears as a normal toilet until you roll
him on the ground and then his eyes and
mouth appear. This was a Kenner original
design.

**The Real Ghostbusters Bad-to-the-Bone
Ghost**
Bad-to-the-Bone was a skeleton who
would open his rib cage to trap one of the
Ghostbusters. The head of the Ghostbuster
would press up and activate the jaw
drop and eye bulge on the Skeleton. This
original Kenner design remains a personal
favorite of mine.

The Real Ghostbusters Bug-Eye Ghost
This purple ghost would shoot a giant eyeball from his forehead when squeezed. One of the early ghost releases from Kenner, this one was an original design.

The Real Ghostbusters Green Ghost with Proton Pack
This version of Slimer is the closest that Kenner produced to an in-scale size. He features action features like bug-out eyes and a dropping jaw. This version features Slimer as one of the Ghostbusters, with a 'no-ghost' logo on his arm and a Proton Pack on his back. There are two color variations of this figure, one with a red pack and one with a blue pack.

The Real Ghostbusters Monsters
Kenner released six figures in this line, all based on movie monsters. The Wolfman Monster, the Dracula Monster, the Frankenstein Monster, the Mummy Monster, the Zombie Monster and the Quasimodo Monster. The toys would all display an action pose when their legs were squeezed.

The Real Ghostbusters Haunted Humans
This line of figures included six human characters that would morph into creepy ghosts. The ghosts include Granny Gross, X-Cop Ghost, Mail Fraud Ghost, Tombstone Tackle Ghost, Terror Trash Ghost and Hard Hat Horror Ghost.

The Real Ghostbusters Mini Traps
This ghostly duo was released alongside the Fright Features toy line. Kids could open the toys' mouths and, once a Ghostbuster made the mistake of stepping on one of their tongues, their jaws would come crashing down, like a bear trap.

The Real Ghostbusters Finger Pop Fiends
The Finger Pop Fiends were a cool new take on an existing Kenner toy line. The Finger Pops were a popular Kenner toy in the late 1970s and early 1980s. Kenner sold Finger Pops, little Styrofoam cylinders, by themselves originally and later with a rubber squeeze gun. The pops would shoot from the gun when pressure was applied, or by themselves when kids would squeeze them hard between their fingers. Kenner also sold refills of the pops. The idea was for the pops to be sold with plastic ghosts that fit around them. There were three color variations of the three fiends.

The Real Ghostbusters Ecto-Plazm Ghosts
Kenner sold three colors of Ecto-Plazm on
shelves. The added bonus was that each
container came packed with a random
ghost. There were twenty-five ghosts in all,
many of which were just color variations.
A complete set of these is beyond difficult
to come by.

The Real Ghostbusters Mini Goopers
This set of ghosts, named Stomach Stuff
and Brain Matter, include a packed-in
half-size carton of Ecto-Plazm. The Kenner
designed ghosts each open up to hold one
ounce of the Ecto-Plazm.

**The Real Ghostbusters Pull Speed Ahead
Ghost**
One of the biggest gimmicks in toys back
in the 1970s and 1980s was rip cords. Add
to that shooting sparks, and this ghost had
it all! Kids just needed to insert the spooky
rip cord, yank it out and let him go.

The Real Ghostbusters Brain Blaster Ghost
This was one of the more off-the-wall ghost designs that Kenner came up with. Brain Blaster came with four pink ghosts that made up his brain matter. When you wheeled him along the ground, the menacing little pieces of brain would jump up and attack.

The Real Ghostbusters Boo-Zooka with Boo-Lets (Mini Shooter)
This Kenner designed ghost shoots two little ghosts – just load up his mouth and squeeze.

The Real Ghostbusters Gobblin' Goblins: Nasty Neck
One of the larger toys in the 'Gobblin' Goblins' line, this guy was released later in the Kenner toy line. You can just pull on his neck and it expands.

The Real Ghostbusters Gobblin' Goblins:
Terror Tongue
Terror Tongue is one of the more interesting of the 'Gobblin' Goblins'. He begins as a cute little rolled-up ghost and unrolls to reveal a more menacing ghost.

The Real Ghostbusters Gobblin' Goblins:
Terrible Teeth
This larger ghost from the 'Gobblin' Goblins' line has a giant mouth with which to chomp the Ghostbusters. The teeth are rubber, so you can chomp the giant jaws down on your Ghostbusters, trapping them.

The Real Ghostbusters Gooper Ghost:
Squisher
The Goopers were Kenner designed ghosts made from hard plastic. The packed-in Ecto-Plazm could be used to ooze slime all over a Ghostbuster, in this case from the ghost's nostrils and mouth!

27

The Real Ghostbusters Gooper Ghost:
Sludge Bucket
Sludge Bucket was a Kenner design
made completely of a hard plastic. He
has a tongue that can be manipulated in
conjunction with packed-in Ecto-Plazm
to blow a bubble over a Ghostbuster to
trap him.

The Real Ghostbusters Gooper Ghost:
Green Ghost
One of the issues that the Kenner toy line
ignored was scale, and this Slimer toy was
no exception. He was a giant-sized version
of Slimer that could 'slime' a Ghostbuster
by oozing packed-in Ecto-Plazm out of
his mouth from his Proton-Pack-looking
backpack. One nice feature is that his
sculpt is far more on-model to the *Real
Ghostbusters* version of the character.

The Real Ghostbusters Gooper Ghost:
Banshee Bomber
This Gooper was another Kenner
design molded from hard plastic. Kids
could make his wings flap and fill him
with packed-in Ecto-Plazm to drop on
unsuspecting Ghostbusters on the ground
below!

The Real Ghostbusters Ecto-1 Vehicle
The Ecto-1 vehicle was released alongside the initial wave of toys in 1986. The car comes packed with an orange ghost, 'Swiveling Blaster Seat' and 'Ghost Claw'.

The Real Ghostbusters Ecto-1A Vehicle
The Ecto-1A was released the same year that *Ghostbusters II* hit theaters, 1989. The car was exactly the same as the original Ecto-1 release, but with updated stickers.

The Real Ghostbusters Ecto-2
Vehicle
The Ecto-2 was a vehicle that
was heavily used in *The Real
Ghostbusters* cartoon, showing up in
a total of twenty episodes. The toy
was a good likeness of the animated
version, but it featured only one
seat, while the cartoon version was
a two-seater.

The Real Ghostbusters Ecto-3
Vehicle
The Ecto-3 vehicle was featured
in the cartoon, as well, but the
similarities end with the name. The
toy version was vastly different
from the animated version. The toy
featured giant paddles to catch the
'Galloping Ghoul Ghost', which came
packed with the vehicle.

The Real Ghostbusters Ecto-500
The Ecto-500 was a smaller go-cart
scale vehicle that included twin
ghost grabbers and a 'Demon
Dasher Ghost'!

The Real Ghostbusters Ghost Sweeper
The Ghost Sweeper was one of the more unorthodox vehicles that Kenner produced. It was basically a street sweeper for catching ghosts. The vehicle included rotating sweepers and the 'Street Creeper Ghost'.

The Real Ghostbusters Ecto-Bomber
The Ecto-Bomber vehicle was the first and only airplane that Kenner introduced into the toy line. The plane featured missiles, a grabber claw and 'Flyer Ghost'.

The Real Ghostbusters Highway Haunter
Highway Haunter was the first vehicle that Kenner produced for the line that was completely off-model from the cartoon. The car is basically a VW Bug that changes to reveal a mantis-style 'Highway Haunter Ghost' hidden inside. The concept for the ghost does resemble Murray the Mantis, who was a giant mantis featured in season two of the cartoon.

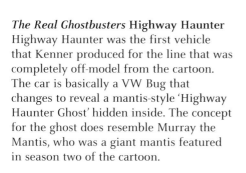

The Real Ghostbusters Haunted Vehicles: Air Sickness

This is one of two 'Haunted Vehicles' produced by Kenner. This one features a humanoid pilot on a one-person aircraft, which transforms into the ghost 'Air Sickness'.

The Real Ghostbusters Haunted Vehicles: Wicked Wheelie

Kenner produced two vehicles in the 'Haunted Vehicles' series. These were vehicles that came equipped with a humanoid driver who is actually a ghost in disguise. This particular one was a motorcycle and driver, which both transform into scary ghosts.

The Real Ghostbusters Firehouse Headquarters

The Ghostbusters Firehouse Headquarters Playset was released in 1997, as the toy line expanded into more ghosts and vehicles. The set included the 'Ghost Pursuit' fire pole, 'Goop Grate', 'Ghost Containment' unit and trap for storing ghosts. The set also featured a 5 oz can of the Ecto-Plazm gel. Fun fact: the Firehouse Headquarters Playset is a particular favorite of Dan Aykroyd. He told me that he actually has about six of them hidden around in various barns on his property!

The Real Ghostbusters Firehouse Headquarters vs *Police Academy* 'The Precinct Police Station'

These two very similar looking playsets were produced by Kenner in the 1980s. It was often thought that the later Police Academy playset was a redeco of the Real Ghostbusters Firehouse but, as you can see by this picture, that is clearly not the case, although some inspiration for the design may very well have come from Ghostbusters. Kenner was known for re-releasing playsets, as seen in the case of the *Return of the Jedi* Ewok Village and the *Robin Hood: Prince of Thieves* Sherwood Forest playset.

The Real Ghostbusters GhostZapper Roleplay Toy

The Kenner GhostZapper was the first roleplay weapon to be released in stores. This chunky kids' version of the Proton Pack Nutrona Wand served as a noisemaker and projector. There was an offer for a second mail-away film cartridge with 'six more wacky ghost images to zap!' Kids had to send in $2.49 to get hold of the refill.

The Real Ghostbusters GhostPopper

This air-powered nerf-style gun from Kenner came packed with three cardboard targets and six foam bullets. The design was again based on the Proton Pack Nutrona Wand.

The Real Ghostbusters Ghost Trap

The Ghost Trap from Kenner was one of the more cartoon-accurate roleplay toys. The trap featured a glow-in-the-dark ghost and trap doors. The trap worked through air press by stomping on the trigger, just as seen in the cartoon. The trap also had a molded piece on the back that would allow it to be clipped onto a belt.

The Real Ghostbusters Ghost Spooker

The electronic Ghost Spooker was designed by Kenner toys to look like the Ghost Trap, but was in fact simply a voice modulator toy that would make your voice high or low to make spooky sounds. 'Electronically makes your voice sound like scary ghosts!'

The Real Ghostbusters **Ecto-Goggles and Ecto-Popper**

This set included a pair of Ecto-Goggles and an Ecto-Popper gun, modeled after the Nutrona Blaster, which can shoot four soft foam pops up to 6 feet away. The Ecto-Goggles have holders on each side to store the foam pops. The set also includes a Stay Puft cardboard target, the same one that was included with the GhostPopper.

The Real Ghostbusters **Proton Pack**

The Kenner roleplay Proton Pack included the pack, tube that connects to the Nutrona Blaster gun with yellow foam attachment, P.K.E. meter, armband and ID card.

The Real Ghostbusters Ecto-Charger Pack
This toy was the Kenner version of the
Slime Blower from *Ghostbusters II*.

The Real Ghostbusters Nutrona Blaster
This Kenner Nutrona Blaster toy came
with a green foam 'Nutrona Ray', which
could turn with a dial on the side of the
gun to 'Zap Ghosts'.

The Real Ghostbusters Rapid Fire
Ecto-Blaster
This gun came later in the Kenner toy line.
The Ecto-Blaster would quickly fire the
four soft-tip darts that came packed in the
toy at one of the cut-out cardboard ghost
targets.

The Real Ghostbusters Ghost Grab-A-Meter
The Kenner Ghost Grab-A-Meter was another late release in the line. Kids could shoot a dart at a 'ghost' enemy and then activate the grabber jaws to capture it.

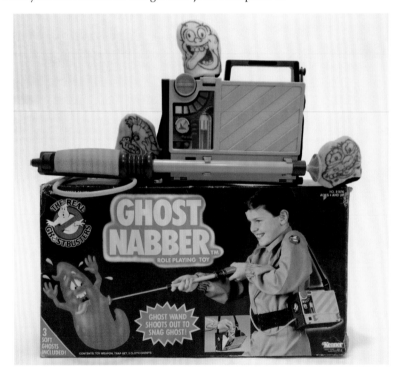

The Real Ghostbusters Ghost Nabber
The Ghost Nabber roleplay toy was one of the few from this toy line for which Kenner drew inspiration from the original film. Peter Venkman can be seen using a similar device in Dana Barrett's apartment early on in the film. This toy came with three soft ghosts to 'nab' with the extendable wand.

The Real Ghostbusters WaterZapper

The WaterZapper was the roleplay toy with a concept that would have been the least effective to ghosts, but perhaps one of the most fun for kids. Kenner made a simple pump-and-shoot water gun.

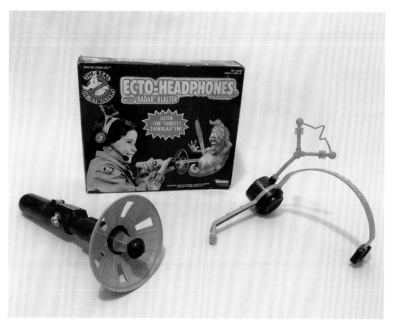

The Real Ghostbusters Ecto-Headphones with Radar Blaster

The Ecto-Headphones come with a spinning antenna that lets you hear a 'ghost-tracking sound'. The accompanying Radar Blaster includes a special 'stun dart' to shoot at a cut-out ghost target.

Stay Puft Marshmallow Man Plush and Green Ghost Puppet
These two items are the only plush produced by Kenner for the toy line. The Stay Puft plush includes glow-in-the-dark elements. The Slimer plush is a hand-puppet.

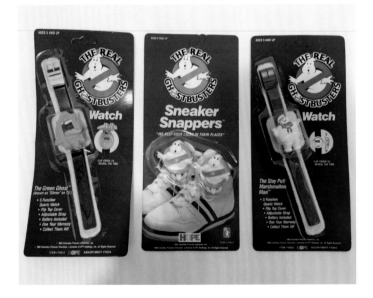

Slimer Watch, Stay Puft Marshmallow Man Watch and Sneaker Snappers
These three accessories were produced by the HOPE company. The shoe charms and watch heads are nicely sculpted renditions. The digital watch heads both open up to reveal the time. The shoe charms are a sign of times that have long passed, but represents a huge fad of the 1980s and part of the 1990s.

Assorted items: Dancing Slimer FM Radio, View Master, View Master Reels, Plaster Molding Set, Action Figure Collector Case, Dodge in the Dark Driving Game.

The Real Ghostbusters 100-Piece Puzzles
These eight 100-piece puzzles represent a full set of what Milton Bradley produced for *The Real Ghostbusters* in the 1980s. The various action scenes depicted include the Ghostbusters fighting various ghosts and the popular Slimer character looking on in all but one design.

The Real Ghostbusters Pencil Box, Night Light, Yo-Yo, Slime Protection Poncho, Handheld Game and Misc. McDonald's Happy Meal School Items (also pictured classic Ghostbusters Four-Piece Juice Glass Set)
The yo-yo craze came back briefly in the 1980s and Spectra Star took the opportunity to release a series of licensed yo-yos, including Mario, Ninja Turtles, Batman and, of course, Ghostbusters. This 'No Ghost' logo yo-yo was the only Ghostbusters design that they produced.

The Real Ghostbusters Magazine

These seasonal magazines were released by Welsh Publishing Group from 1989 through to 1991, for a total of seven issues. They were released in conjunction with the *Ghostbusters II* feature film, at the height of Ghostbusters popularity. The issues included Summer 1989, Fall 1989, Winter 1990, Spring 1990, Summer 1990, Fall 1990, and Winter 1991.

The Real Ghostbusters Colorforms and Glow-in-the-Dark Colorforms Play Sets

Colorforms play sets were a staple of the 1980s, with many of the various licensed franchises getting a set. *The Real Ghostbusters* was fortunate enough to get two sets, one standard and one larger glow-in-the-dark set.

The Real Ghostbusters Pocket Gumball Dispenser, *The Real Ghostbusters* Jelly Candy and *The Real Ghostbusters* Gumball Machine

These candy-related items include a mini gumball machine with gumballs, jelly candies and a gumball machine. Candy tie-in product was a very popular staple of the 1980s.

The Real Ghostbusters Party/Novelty Items: Screaming Ghost, Search Set and Ghost Extinguisher

These three items, all produced by Ja-Ru, were intended as joke/novelty/party items. They are essentially kazoos, cheap plastic binoculars and a water-squirting fire extinguisher.

***The Real Ghostbusters* Magic Slate, Shaving Kit and Pinball Game**
Golden books produced this fun magic slate. Kids can write whatever they like with the included pen and then lift the page to erase it. The kids' faux shaving kit is a popular novelty item to this day. The pinball game was produced by Ja-Ru.

***The Real Ghostbusters* Shrinky Dinks and Glow-in-the-Dark Shrinky Dinks Deluxe Activity Set**
The first set pictured is Milton Bradley Shrinky Dinks. These are plastic cut-outs that you color and bake in the oven to shrink and harden. The second set is a Colorforms produced Shrinky Dinks set; this one is glow-in-the-dark, a popular gimmick of the 1980s. Colorforms had licensed the ability to make Shrinky Dink sets in 1981 and throughout the 1980s produced over fifty sets, including this one.

The Real Ghostbusters Locker Bag, *The Real Ghostbusters* Tin and *The Real Ghostbusters* Stay Puft Keychain

The locker bag concept was popular in the eighties and nineties. The set included items like tissues, soap, a cup and other hygiene goodies. The keychain was produced by a company called HOPE.

The Real Ghostbusters Gym Bag and Backpack

The miniature gym bag was an item often produced for kids in the 1980s. This particular one includes only Egon, Peter, Ray and Slimer. The backpack is a great mimic of the Proton Pack. I wouldn't mind having one of those in adult size!

The Real Ghostbusters Streamer Kite, Windsock, Party Supplies and Static Stick-Ons
The Streamer Kite was produced by Spectra Star, as was the windsock. The Hallmark and C.A. Reed produced party supplies are among the most-desired Ghostbusters collectables. I get dozens of emails every week with parents looking for Ghostbusters party supplies for their kids. Pictured here are party stickers, paper plates (both sizes) and loot (treat) bags. The two Slimer static clings pictured, produced by Dakin, came in a variety of styles beyond what is shown here.

The Real Ghostbusters Storybooks
These half-size storybooks were offered through book orders and at limited retail stores. These books are listed as number two and number three in a series of twelve. This series can be a bit of a mystery; it's uncertain if the other titles were ever produced.

46

**The Real Ghostbusters
in Revenge of the Ghosts
Story and Sticker Book**
This half-size storybook
included twelve collector
stickers inside. These were
offered through school
book orders and limited
retail outlets.

**The Real Ghostbusters
Storybooks**
These storybooks offered
original tales and artwork
to tie-in to the cartoon.

**The Real Ghostbusters
Comic Books**
NOW Comics produced
Ghostbusters comic books
from 1988 to 1993. The
company released two
volumes of the series,
with twenty-eight issues
in volume one and four
issues in volume two. There
was also a 1992 and a 1993
annual. Pictured are volume
one, issues number twelve
and fifteen, and the 1992
annual.

47

The Real Ghostbusters Stay Puft Night Light FM Radio
This FM radio features the Stay Puft Marshmallow Man molded in rubber on the top. The radio includes a power adaptor and a built-in nightlight.

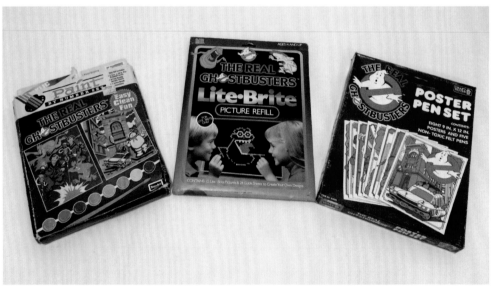

The Real Ghostbusters Paint by Numbers, Lite-Brite Picture Refill and Poster Pen Set
The paint-by-number set included paints, a brush and a couple of pictures to paint, produced by Rose-Art. The Lite-Brite refill came complete with patterns to create Ghostbusters images on the Lite board. The poster pen set came with eight posters to color with the pack-in markers and was produced by Craft House.

The Real Ghostbusters Kids' Uniform
These vintage uniforms were produced for kids to roleplay as their favorite Ghostbuster. There were three variant uniforms with various images on the back.

The Real Ghostbusters Suspenders and Hallmark Birthday Sign
Pictured here are both colors of *The Real Ghostbusters* suspenders, red and blue. The sign was sold by Hallmark in their party supply line. The image features Slimer and the message 'Danger Slime Zone'. This sign remains one of my personal favorites.

The Real Ghostbusters Pinball Game
This electronic pinball game, produced by Ideal, includes flashing lights and a ringing bell.

49

The Real Ghostbusters Car Window Static Stick-Ons
These static clings, produced by Marlenn, were reusable stickers intended to be used on the side window of your car. Pictured here are Slimer and 'No Ghost' logo designs.

The Real Ghostbusters Sticker Book and Sticker Packs
The Diamond Publishing and Panini sticker albums have been going strong since the 1980s and the Panini brand can still be found in stores today. The two brands split the marketplace throughout the 1980s. Kids buy the book to place the stickers in and then purchase individual packs to collect them all. These were released for both *The Real Ghostbusters* and *Slimer!* and *The Real Ghostbusters by Diamond*!

The Real Ghostbusters Coloring Books
Golden Books released a number of coloring books for *The Real Ghostbusters* cartoon series.

***The Real Ghostbusters* VHS and BETA Home Video**
Pictured here are VHS and BETA examples of *The Real Ghostbusters* home video media. Beta, or Betamax, was a competing home video medium in the early 1980s. The tapes were smaller than VHS. Releases from Magic Window include *Vol. 1: Knock, Knock/Vol. 2: Play Them Ragtime Boos/Vol. 3: A Fright at the Opera/Vol. 4: Venkman's Ghost Repellers/Vol. 5: The Bird of Kildarby and Other Stories/Vol. 6: The Revenge of Murray the Mantis And Other Stories/Vol. 7: Ghost Fight at the O.K. Corral.* Kid Classics re-released the following, all on VHS: *Vol. 3: A Fright at the Opera and Other Stories/Vol. 5: The Bird of Kildarby And Other Stories/Vol. 6: The Revenge of Murray the Mantis and Other Stories.* A collector's edition of 'Cry Uncle' was also released by Magic Window, originally as a cereal premium.

***Cartoon All-Stars to the Rescue* VHS (featuring Slimer)**
This anti-drug animated feature was produced by McDonalds in the late 1980s. The cartoon featured a slew of popular animated characters from the era, including Michelangelo from *Teenage Mutant Ninja Turtles*, ALF, The Smurfs, Garfield, Winnie the Pooh and Slimer from *The Real Ghostbusters*. The VHS was offered as a free rental in video stores and can be rather difficult to locate on the secondary market. The example shown is new and still sealed in its original plastic.

The Real Ghostbusters Play-Doh Play Set
This play set came packed with special glow-in-the-dark Play-Doh, an Ecto-1 mold and other assorted molds, along with a Ghostbusters themed play mat.

The Real Ghostbusters SpitBalls
These were a popular item for a season back in the 1980s. The spitballs were released by Enertech during the same era that Madballs were gracing store shelves. The little molded character balls could absorb and spit water up to 18 feet.

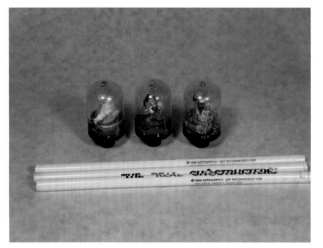

The Real Ghostbusters Pencils with Water Globe Pencil Toppers
Noteworthy released a total of four pencils with toppers in this series. Pictured are Peter Venkman, Slimer and the 'No Ghost' logo. Not pictured is the Stay Puft Marshmallow Man. One disadvantage to these items, as you can see in the picture, is that the liquid in the globes has evaporated in most cases.

**The Real Ghostbusters
Party Supplies**
Hallmark released a
popular line of party
supplies that included party
hats, invitations, thank you
cards, plates, tablecloth,
napkins and cups. Pictured
are invitations, tablecloth
and napkins.

**The Real Ghostbusters
Lunchboxes**
Thermos produced
various designs of *The
Real Ghostbusters* plastic
lunchboxes. These two
were the most prolific. The
lunchboxes were released
in a variety of colors
including orange, red, blue
and purple. Thermos also
released similar *The Real
Ghostbusters* lunchtime
products, including a green
side-snapping lunchbox and
a vinyl soft lunch bag kit.

**The Real Ghostbusters
Metal TV Tray**
These trays were very
popular licensed items
in the 1980s. They were
used to eat meals on while
sitting in front of the
television.

The Real Ghostbusters Ralston Purina Cereal Sales Kit
This very rare sales kit was a folder given to Ralston Purina Cereal sales professionals to use on the road when pitching *The Real Ghostbusters* cereal to stores. The kit includes sales figures, action plans, coupon suggestions and dozens of other sheets and information to use on a sales call. The kit also includes flat, never-assembled hologram cereal boxes.

The Real Ghostbusters Cereal Premium Posters
These two posters were packed in boxes of Ghostbusters cereal. The artwork was provided by NOW Comics artists John Tobias and Cygnet Ash. A bit of trivia: John Tobias would go on to be the co-creator of the popular Mortal Kombat video game franchise over at Midway games.

The Real Ghostbusters Cereal Premium Glow-In-The-Dark Slimer
This in-pack cereal premium was a rubber Slimer that glowed in the dark, along with a contest entry (pictured). These were largely considered throwaway items and can be difficult to find in today's secondary market, especially with the contest entry.

The Real Ghostbusters Hologram Cereal T-Shirt Mail-Away Premium
The Real Ghostbusters cereal did two series of holographic boxes. The second set included a mail-away offer for a matching hologram t-shirt. I had this shirt as a kid and it was extremely cool and very durable.

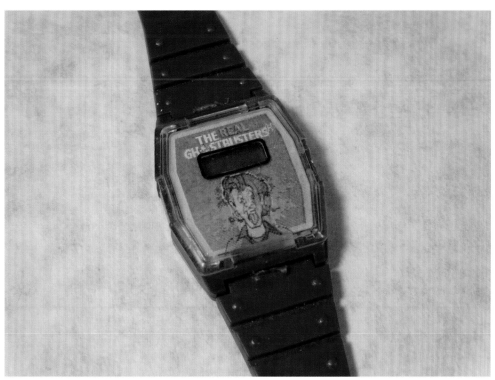

The Real Ghostbusters Mail-Away Watch
This lenticular Peter Venkman watch was offered as a mail-away.

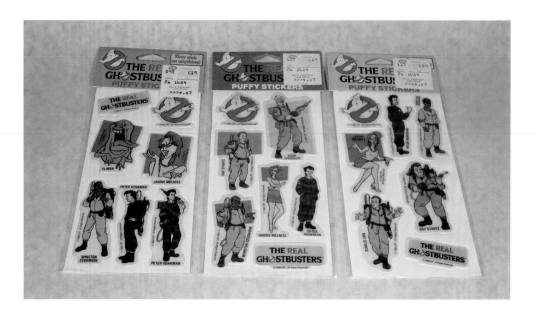

The Real Ghostbusters **Puffy Stickers**
Few items in the 1980s were as hot as stickers ... especially puffy stickers. These three sets were released with images from *The Real Ghostbusters* cartoon.

The Real Ghostbusters **Happy Meal (Bike Set)**
There were two *The Real Ghostbusters* McDonald's Happy Meal sets released in the 1980s. This one was full of gear for a kid's bicycle, including a Slimer horn, water bottle and a siren.

The Real Ghostbusters Happy Meal (School Set)
This McDonald's Happy Meal includes various school supply items. Included in this set was a Stay Puft Marshmallow Man notepad, 'No Ghost' logo eraser, Slimer pencil topper, Stay Puft Marshmallow Man pencil sharpener and a pencil case with a ruler. (Pencil topper and ruler not pictured.)

The Real Ghostbusters Telephone
This touchtone telephone has the design of the 'no ghost' logo.

The Real Ghostbusters Bed Sheets
This sheet set featured *The Real Ghostbusters* fighting various ghosts on the streets of New York. The set included a fitted sheet, top sheet and pillow case.

The Real Ghostbusters Hi-C Ecto Cooler Drink
Hi-C produced the Slimer themed Ecto Cooler fruit drink until 1997. The drink was released in 46 oz metal cans, juice boxes and, later in the 1990s, plastic gallons. The drink had two designs (both pictured above). These are among the most valuable and desirable collectables in the Ghostbusters world.

The Real Ghostbusters Hi-C Promotional Lunch Bags
These were given out in bags of four (two of each design) at stores as a promotional item when purchasing Hi-C products.

Slimer! and The Real Ghostbusters

Slimer! and The Real Ghostbusters was a sub-series to *The Real Ghostbusters* cartoon that was added in 1988 to the third season of the show. The ABC network expanded the show to a one-hour timeslot that featured a half-hour episode of the standard *Real Ghostbusters* series and then two or three *Slimer!* shorts. The *Slimer!* shorts were geared towards younger kids, with a different animation style and stories that featured *Slimer!* interacting with his various human and animal friends, and avoiding his enemies Professor Dweeb and Manx.

Slimer! and The Real Ghostbusters Sticker Packs
These five-packs of stickers were sold as inserts to the Diamond *Slimer! and The Real Ghostbusters* sticker books.

Slimer! Comic Books
Once Slimer became a wildly popular break-out part of *The Real Ghostbusters* cartoon, he was granted his own spin-off cartoon show. NOW Comics also gave him his own comic book series. NOW produced nineteen issues of the series and one special 3D issue. Pictured are issues four, five, eleven and nineteen.

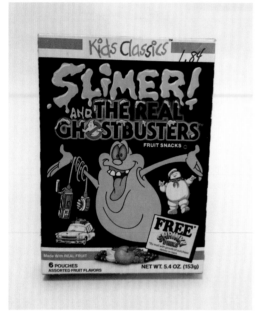

Slimer! and The Real Ghostbusters Fruit Snacks
These fruit snack treats were produced by Kids Classics to promote the *Slimer!* spin-off cartoon. They featured exclusive mail-aways, like Shrinky Dinks.

Slimer! and The Real Ghostbusters Cereal
This cereal was eventually re-branded to represent the Slimer cartoon spin-off.

Chapter Three
Filmation's Ghostbusters

The first time that kids were exposed to the idea of the Ghostbusters was back in 1975 when Filmation produced a Saturday morning live-action television series called *The Ghost Busters*. The series consisted of two slapstick characters, Kong and Spencer, joined by their gorilla friend Tracy. The series featured the bumbling ghost-hunting trio driving around in their run-down jalopy, investigating paranormal disturbances for their clients. The Ghost Busters encountered famous monsters like Frankenstein, the Mummy and even Count Dracula! They would eliminate the spooks with their Ghost De-Materializer gun. The short-lived series ran for a total of fifteen episodes on the CBS network.

When Columbia Pictures developed their *Ghostbusters* film, which was in no way based on the old series, they did pay Filmation a licensing fee to utilize the name. Filmation was a highly successful animation company, producing hit series like *He-Man* and the *Masters of the Universe*, so it would seem logical that, if an animated series were to take place, then Filmation would be the company to handle the project. The film was a raging success and thus Columbia chose to capitalize on that with a syndicated animated series but, of course, we all know that Filmation didn't end up producing the cartoon.

Filmation were already in production to bring their original Ghostbusters concept to an updated cartoon format long before Columbia decided to produce a cartoon based on their film. Lou Scheimer, the head of Filmation, wanted to work with the studio to produce one cartoon based on the film, but it was decided that producing their own series would be less expensive and less hassle. The series was able to maintain the title *Ghostbusters*, while the Columbia version had to adapt the more confusing, and slightly snarky name, *The Real Ghostbusters*.

Filmation's Ghostbusters cartoon ran for one season and enjoyed a total of sixty-five episodes. The cartoon has been met with mixed reviews from fans over the years. There were kids that loved both of the Ghostbusters series, and those that adamantly disliked the Filmation version. All the Ghostheads are entitled to their own opinions on this one but, no matter what your opinion is, there is no denying that the Filmation show is certainly a part of Ghostbusters history.

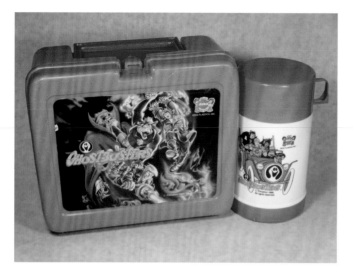

Filmation's Ghostbusters
Lunchbox
This lunchbox, from Deka Plastics, was the only one produced for *Filmation's Ghostbusters*.

Filmation's Ghostbusters
Comic Books
The short-lived *Filmation's Ghostbusters* comic book series ran for only four issues (issues one to three are pictured). It was produced by First Comics. The issues included not only comics, but also coloring and activity pages.

Filmation's Ghostbusters
VHS
A series of VHS releases were produced by Celebrity Just For Kids.

Filmation's Ghostbusters Ghost Buggy with Jake Kong Jr, Eddie Spencer Jr, Traci and Jessica
Action Figures
These action figures were produced for the mass market by Schaper. The figures and the Ghost
Buggy are very difficult to come across on the secondary market and fetch a rather high price.

Filmation's Ghostbusters Bone Troller with Prime Evil, Haunter, Fib Face, Mysteria, Scared
Stiff and Brat-A-Rat Action Figures
These villain figures were produced by Schaper, including Prime Evil's Bone Troller, which is
pulled right out of the cartoon series.

Filmation's Ghostbusters Time Hopper with Futura Action Figure
The Time Hopper is another of the vehicles produced by Schaper. The Futura figure was sold separately.

Filmation's Ghostbusters Scare Scooter
The Scare Scooter vehicle, by Schaper toys, is pictured here along with the evil Fangster action figure (sold separately). Fangster can be seen riding this vehicle in episodes of the cartoon.

64

Filmation's Ghostbusters Ghost Command Playset
This playset is the holy grail for any _Filmation's Ghostbusters_ collector. The set has been known to fetch upwards of $1,000 new in the box.

Chapter Four
Ghostbusters II Movie Merchandise

I can still remember the moment that I learned there was going to be a live-action sequel to my beloved *Ghostbusters*. This was an era without the internet, when a kid wasn't really in the know about upcoming releases unless you were lucky enough to see a preview before a film, an ad on television or read something in a magazine. I was ten years old and home alone while my parents had their date night. Our clunky console television was on, playing a movie of the week and, during the commercial break, the first trailer for *Ghostbusters II* came on and I couldn't believe my eyes. It was a dream come true. I set up my VCR to record the commercial the next time it played, but alas it never played again that night.

Fan feelings about the second Ghostbusters film are mixed, to say the least.

***Ghostbusters II* Plastic Drink Mug and AMC Theaters Plastic Cup**
The first cup is a *Ghostbusters II* movie drink mug. This plastic cup was available in 1989 at select AMC theaters and can prove to be difficult to find in today's secondary marketplace.

Ghostbusters II Trading Cards
This trading card line, produced by Topps, featured a set of cards and stickers. Each set came packed with gum, as was customary at the time. Pictured here is the full set of cards, a few closed packs and the poster that came packed in every box for the retailer to display.

Ghostbusters II Cereal and Premium Collectable Movie Mystery Records
Pictured here is a box of the *Ghostbusters II* edition of the Ralston Ghostbusters cereal. Also shown are the gold and silver edition collectable Ghostbusters mystery records. These records were packed in to cereal boxes as a prize. The idea was that you play the record to see if you are a contest winner. The contest was to win the chance to meet a real Ghostbuster, whatever that meant. These flimsy records were rather breakable and therefore were often disposed of.

Ghostbusters II **Lunchbox**
This plastic lunchbox featured the movie logo, Slimer and the Ecto-1A, along with the New York City Twin Towers in the background.

Ghostbusters II **Slimer Candy Container**
This plastic Slimer candy container held sweet-tart-like candies.

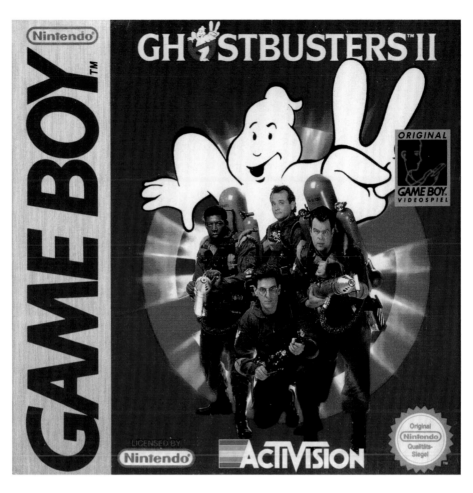

Ghostbusters II Video Game
Activision developed the *Ghostbusters II* movie video game and released it on both the NES and original Gameboy platforms.

Ghostbusters II Hi-C Stencils
The Hi-C Ecto Cooler was a very popular drink among kids of the 1980s and remains a widely desired cult hit to this day. These five stencils were in-pack promotional items with Ecto Cooler to promote *Ghostbusters II*.

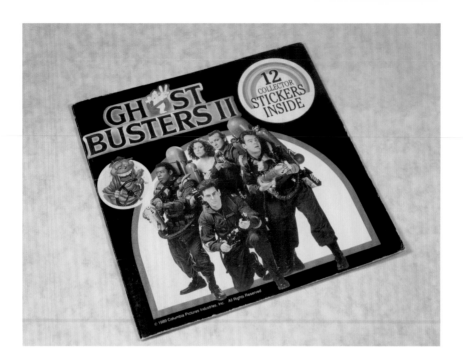

Ghostbusters II **Movie Sticker Book**
These half-size books were popular in book orders and were available at some limited retail outlets. The books included twelve collector stickers to place on each page of the book.

Ghostbusters II **Activity Books**
This series of *Ghostbusters II* activity books was released in 1989 to accompany the movie. The books came in various colors and sizes, but always with fun activities. (Not all versions are pictured.)

Ghostbusters II Movie Tie-In Books
These various tie-in books to the sequel film include an oversized storybook with full-color pictures, the movie novelization, a more kid-friendly version of the novelization and a joke, puzzle and game book. The kid-friendly version was not only on store shelves, but was also offered through school book orders.

Ghostbusters II Hardee's Drink Cup, Collector Poster and Pencil Box
Hardee's touted itself as the 'Official *Ghostbusters II* Headquarters' during the theatrical release of the 1989 sequel. This promotion took place during an era when fast food restaurants gave out more durable collector cups. This plastic Ghostbusters cup prominently features the *Ghostbusters II* logo. The collector poster folds out into a poster and also has cut-out coupons on it. The white plastic box as a kids' meal option in some markets.

71

Set of Four *Ghostbusters II* Hardee's Kids' Meal Boxes with Stickers
These four plastic boxes came packed with a sticker sheet and a toy catalog. The versions included Slimer, Ecto-1, Proton Pack and a ghost. A full set of these can be rare, especially since the boxes are very brittle and crack easily.

Ghostbusters II Mail-Away Hat
A Hardee's/Kenner promotion in conjunction with *The Real Ghostbusters* toy line offered fans either a $2 rebate by mail or this *Ghostbusters II* white-and-blue trucker-style hat. All you had to do is send in UPC proofs of purchase for three *Real Ghostbusters* toys.

Ghostbusters II Hardee's Ghost Blasters
These noisemakers could be purchased for $1.79 each; they came in red, white, gray and black.

Chapter Five
The Extreme Ghostbusters Cartoon

Ghostbusters had been an all but dead franchise throughout the majority of the 1990s, until Sony Pictures Television decided to try and breathe new life into the once-lucrative characters. In 1996 it was announced that an all-new cartoon series, then titled *Super Ghostbusters*, was in development. Animated shows were still all the rage in the glory days of the 1990s, so it was extremely reasonable to test the marketplace with a cartoon before daring to fork over the big money needed for a third installment in the live-action feature film franchise.

One of the key elements that made *Extreme Ghostbusters* not only a great show, but also an underrated piece of the Ghostbusters franchise, is that it was an actual continuation of *The Real Ghostbusters* cartoon from the 1980s. The show featured a return of an older Egon and Janine, voiced by original voice actors Maurice LaMarche and Pat Musick. There were various crossover elements and references to the original animated series, including a two-part episode that featured the other three Ghostbusters returning to action, sporting voice actors from *The Real Ghostbusters*.

Extreme Ghostbusters debuted in September 1997 and was treated to a whopping forty episodes during its one and only season. The show faced various distribution issues around the country, with many marketplaces opting out of carrying the series.

Trendmasters managed to produce the first ever Sam Hain figure, despite his not being included in the cartoon, except during the introduction. One of the key Extreme Ghostbusters, the wheelchair-bound jock Garrett Miller, never got the plastic treatment. There was a prototype action figure produced, but it was never released to the marketplace.

The *Extreme Ghostbusters* cartoon didn't last long on the air, so it wasn't heavily merchandised. There are a few items that are not pictured in this chapter, such as three different VHS releases and a ride-on Ecto-1 machine.

Extreme Ghostbusters Ecto-1 Vehicle, Action Figures and KFC Kids' Meal Toys
Trendmasters produced an all-new version of Ecto-1 for their *Extreme Ghostbusters* toy line. Also pictured here are the standard Kylie, Egon and Eduardo and the deluxe Roland action figure. There were two toy lines released by Trendmasters, the standard figures and the deluxe figures.

Extreme Ghostbusters Unproduced Garrett Miller Action Figure Prototype
This is a rare look at the prototype created, but never released, by Trendmasters. (From the collection of Jonathan Shyman.)

Extreme Ghostbusters **Mouth Critter and Sam Hain Ghosts Action Figures**
These two ghosts were produced by Trendmasters for the *Extreme Ghostbusters* toy line in 1997.
Also included in the line, but not pictured, are Slimer and the House Ghost.

Extreme Ghostbusters **Unproduced Sam Hain Action Figure Prototype**
Pictured here on the right is the retail version of Sam Hain that was released. On the left is a
rare one-of-a-kind prototype that was produced for photography and to show at Toy Fair. (From
the collection of Jonathan Shyman.)

Extreme Ghostbusters **Ghost Grabbin Gyro-Copter with Extreme Ecto Edition Roland**
This vehicle/action figure pack was released only in the foreign marketplace and in very limited
quantities. (From the collection of Jonathan Shyman.)

Extreme Ghostbusters **Ghost Blastin Buster Bike with Extreme Ecto Edition Eduardo**
This vehicle/action figure pack was released only in the foreign marketplace and in very limited
quantities. (From the collection of Jonathan Shyman.)

Extreme Ghostbusters Roleplay Toys

Trendmasters continued the rich tradition set by Kenner in the 1980s and released a handful of roleplay toys in conjunction with their *Extreme Ghostbusters* toy line. Pictured here are the Ghost Trap, Plasma Blaster and the Proton Pack with Plasma Blaster. These roleplay weapons tend to be rather rare and nearly impossible to come by casually. They can be found online for sale at a premium price.

Extreme Ghostbusters Video Games

Releases included a Nintendo Gameboy Color game, _Extreme Ghostbusters_: _Code Ecto-1_, Nintendo Gameboy Advance game and the _Extreme Ghostbusters: The Ultimate Invasion_ Playstation game. The latter was released for the original Playstation console, but only in the United Kingdom.

Chapter Six
The Modern Era

The *Extreme Ghostbusters* cartoon gave us just one season and after that collectors would find themselves in a drought of toys. We lived out the rest of the 1990s without any real showings of merchandise and, as the millennium began, things weren't looking any better. Then, one special day in 2003, I remember walking into a Hot Topic store in a local shopping mall and my gaze was met with a glorious sight – new Ghostbusters merchandise!

The Hot Topic era gave us t-shirts, postcards, stickers and more based on the original 1984 feature film. This was the beginning of our modern era and our obsession with retro and nostalgia.

The next bits of merchandise were slow moving, with small glimpses of light in the way of a comic book series from 88MPH Comics and a book that would become infamous among fans. A novel based on the Ghostbusters, titled *Ghostbusters: The Return*, was released in 2004 by iBooks and author Sholly Fisch. I had the pleasure of interviewing Sholly for GhostbustersCollector.com years ago and he had some interesting insights about the book and the state of the franchise that I'd like to share with you:

iBooks originally intended to publish a set of three books, and maybe more if the sales were good enough. The idea was that the books would carry on the Ghostbusters story, much like the *Star Wars* or *Star Trek* series of novels.

But, alas, it was not to be. The first major pitfall came when Barnes & Noble decided that Ghostbusters was a 'dead property'; they didn't think a novel based on a twenty-year-old movie would sell. As a result, they decided to sell the novel through their website, but not shelve it in their stores – and, considering how much of the market Barnes & Noble controls, that was pretty much the kiss of death for book sales.

As bad as that was, the next pitfall was far more tragic: Byron Preiss, the owner and publisher of iBooks, was killed in a car accident. Without Byron, the company soon went under, along with the Ghostbusters license and the back stock of books that were sitting in a warehouse someplace. That's why the novel is so hard to find now. The Barnes & Noble issue kept the print run low, and because iBooks went out of business, I'm pretty sure a whole bunch of the printed copies never got distributed at all.

The biggest jump in merchandise would come in 2009 when Diamond Select Toys and Mattel, both having recognized the demand in the marketplace, began to produce new Ghostbusters toys! There have been a number of companies that have since jumped on board, producing merchandise purely based on a cult following of fans and collectors, rather than any active cartoon or film series, including Funko and Atari.

I have carefully selected what I feel is a fine sampling of the modern era of Ghostbusters collectables for this chapter.

Hot Topic Ghostbusters Merchandise
In 2003 Hot Topic stores carried a line of merchandise inspired by the original 1984 *Ghostbusters* film. Pictured above are the postcards, stickers, air freshener, button and a patch. Not-pictured items in this line include Stay Puft Marshmallow Man, Terror Dog and Ghostbusters logo ringer shirts.

Ghostbusters: The Video Game

This Atari developed third-person-shooter video game helped to revitalize the Ghostbusters franchise long before any reboot films were planned. Gamers could play as 'The Rookie' and learn how to be a Ghostbuster. The game featured the voices of Dan Aykroyd, Harold Ramis, Bill Murray and Ernie Hudson. The game was so popular that the original ghosts created for the game were even immortalized as Minimates. *Ghostbusters: The Video Game* sold well over a million copies in the first year of release. The game was released on the PS2, PS3, PSP, Xbox 360, Wii, Nintendo DS and Windows computer formats.

Ghostbusters: The Video Game **Pre-Order Cards**

These cool pre-order cards could reserve players a copy of the Ghostbusters game on different formats for the low price of just $1. Many savvy collectors picked up these cards to hold onto.

The Real Ghostbusters **Complete Series DVD Set**
Time Life released this epic box set in 2009. The set includes all five seasons of the series, a bonus disc, book and a collectable Ghostbusters Firehouse case.

Ghostbusters Movie Claw Machine Plush
Sugar Loaf produced a line of claw machine plush toys in recent years including the four Ghostbusters, Slimer and Stay Puft. The plush came in various sizes. Pictured are Peter Venkman, Stay Puft and Slimer.

Ghostbusters Video Slots Promotional T-Shirt
This t-shirt is a rare promotional item produced to advertise the Ghostbusters Video Slots casino game.

Miscellaneous Modern Ghostbusters Collectables: Wallet, Candy Tin, Stay Puft Mini Plush, Sticker and Keychain

Ghostbusters Stay Puft Marshmallows
This novelty box of marshmallows was produced in 2012 by the Parallax Corporation.

Ghostbusters: *Legion* **Comic Book Series**
This comic book series, released in early 2004, was the first to resurrect the Ghostbusters in the modern era. The four-part miniseries, published by 88MPH comics, was a huge hit with fans. There was also a #0 issue that ended up being a San Diego Comic Con exclusive that year.

Ghostbusters Ecto-1 Model
This snap-together model was produced by Polar Lights in 2002.

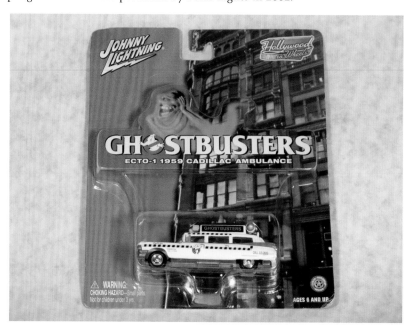

Ghostbusters Ecto-1 Die-Cast Vehicle
Fans with a keen eye will notice right away that, even though Johnny Lightning released this vehicle under the name Ecto-1, it is clearly the *Ghostbusters II* movie Ecto-1A. This car was released under the Hollywood on Wheels series. Johnny Lightning has released a dozen or so various Ecto 1-A die-cast cars over the years in various paint schemes.

Ghostbusters Krispy Kreme Promotion

To help celebrate the thirty-year anniversary of the original *Ghostbusters* film, Krispy Kreme had two special edition Ghostbusters donuts and a plastic donut holes pail that fans could buy. Pictured here is the limited edition dozen donuts box and plastic donut holes pail.

Minimates and Diamond Select Toys

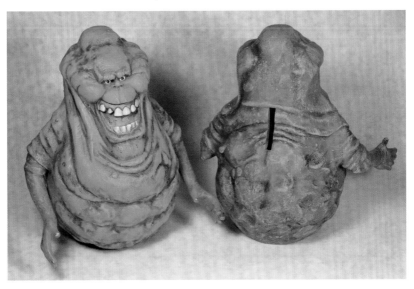

Ghostbusters Slimer Bank

This Slimer bank from Diamond Select Toys is a representation of the character from the original feature film. The great sculpt on this figural bank was by Rudy Garcia. When I spoke to Rudy recently about his work on the bank, he told me that he 'would like to revisit this character some day and cast him in green, translucent silicon.' That would be awesome!

87

Ghostbusters Stay Puft Marshmallow Man Bank and Angry Burnt Stay Puft Bank
Diamond Select Toys produced these wonderfully sculpted representations of the Stay Puft
Marshmallow Man from the original 1984 film.

Ghostbusters Terror Dog Statue
This fantastic Diamond Select Toys 7-inch light-up statue features the Gozer Terror Dog from the
first _Ghostbusters_ feature film. The sculpt was done by Bill Mancuso and the paint application
was done by Jason Wires.

Twenty-Fifth Anniversary Minimate (SDCC giveaway)
In the summer of 2009 Diamond Select Toys surprised fans at the San Diego Comic Con by giving away a special edition Ghostbusters twenty-fifth anniversary all-black Minimate at their booth.

Ghostbusters: The Video Game Minimates Four-Pack
This Amazon.com exclusive pack of Minimates are original ghosts based on the Ghostbusters video game.

Ghostbusters Minimates Box Sets

The Real Ghostbusters Minimates Box Set and Two-Packs

Funko Ghostbusters Product

Ghostbusters Funko POP! Movies Winston Zeddemore Vinyl Figure with Ecto-1 Vehicle; Dr Raymond Stantz Vinyl Figure; Dr Peter Venkman Vinyl Figure; Dr Egon Spengler Vinyl Figure; Slimer Vinyl Figure and 6-inch Super-Sized Stay Puft Marshmallow Man Vinyl Figure

Ghostbusters Funko POP! Movies Stay Domo Vinyl Figure, Domo Ghostbusters Vinyl Figure and Domo Slimer Vinyl Figure

Ghostbusters Funko Vinyl Idolz Dr Raymond Stantz, Dr Peter Venkman and Dr. Egon Spengler

Ghostbusters Funko Vinyl Sugar Dorbz Vinyl Collectable Ray Stantz, Egon Spengler, Peter Venkman and Winston Zeddemore

Mattel Ghostbusters Toys

Ghostbusters **San Diego Comic Con Exclusive Egon Spengler Action Figure and Peter Venkman Action Figure**
The first release from the 6-inch Mattel line was the 'slimed' Egon. He came packed with Slimer, as well. The Peter Venkman is another figure from the first release of the figures. The Ghostbusters movie figure line included the four Ghostbusters with various ghosts and never-before-seen action figures like Walter Peck (packed with the Containment Unit), Vinz Clortho (packed with Terror Dog mask) and Dana Barrett as Zuul.

The Real Ghostbusters **Retro-Action Figures**
Mattel tried their hand at producing *The Real Ghostbusters* figures, but, rather than travel down the route that Kenner had gone before, they decided to produce a more unorthodox route and produce figures that were more doll-like, as a retro nod to the Mego toys of the 1970s. Pictured are the four Ghostbusters that were released to retail outlets like Toys R Us.

The Real Ghostbusters Retro-Action San Diego Comic Con Exclusive Peter Venkman Figure

The line debuted at San Diego Comic Con with a special edition Peter Venkman figure from the 'Citizen Ghost' episode of the cartoon series. The episode shows the aftermath of the original 1984 *Ghostbusters* movie and explains the colorful suits used in the cartoon. In the episode, the brown suits that the Ghostbusters wore were ecto-charged and became haunted, coming alive with green glowing ghostly versions of the Ghostbusters. Pictured is the standard con-exclusive figure – not pictured is a green glowing ghost version.

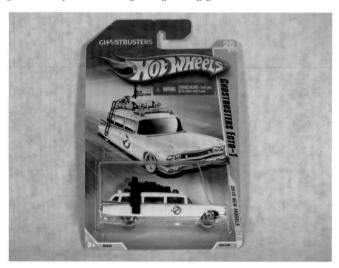

Ghostbusters Ecto-1 1:64 scale Die-Cast Hot Wheels Vehicle

This was the first Ghostbusters release from Hot Wheels. They have since released various versions of the Ecto-1 and Ecto 1-A in a number of sizes. There have also been redeco versions of the cars sold in special Halloween editions. They have recently released a die-cast version of the Ecto-1 from *The Real Ghostbusters*. When I asked Dan Aykroyd which Ghostbusters toy was his favorite, he specifically mentioned the 1:18 scale Hot Wheels Elite Die-Cast Ecto-1: 'For me the Mattel massive scale metal Ecto-1 is a magnificent example, which combines the sophistication of an art piece suitable for any great mantel or power table with the full toyetic satisfaction and joy that an Ecto-1 brings to any party.'